IMAGES
of America

PILOT POINT

Surveyor G. W. Newcome laid out the town of Pilot Point on Christmas day in 1853 along with James Pierson, heir to the original land grantee. The survey was recorded on June 28, 1854, in the records of Denton County, and Pierson proceeded to sell lots to settlers and merchants. This map of the town square is from the Sanborn Map of 1885 showing the various businesses that operated at that time. (Courtesy of Elwood Branum.)

ON THE COVER: Cowboys and horses were a vital part of the economy of Pilot Point around the dawn of the 20th century. This photograph, taken in 1910 on South Washington Street just south of the square, reflects that importance. Pictured here from left to right are Earl McNabb, Jim Pitner, Bill Phiney, Louis Landenborn, and Nye Phiney. (Courtesy of Clifton Irick.)

IMAGES
of America

PILOT POINT

Jay Melugin

ARCADIA
PUBLISHING

Published by Arcadia Publishing
Charleston SC, Chicago IL, Portsmouth NH, San Francisco CA

Library of Congress Control Number: 2009920419

For all general information contact Arcadia Publishing at:
Telephone 843-853-2070
Fax 843-853-0044
E-mail sales@arcadiapublishing.com
For customer service and orders:
Toll-Free 1-888-313-2665

Visit us on the Internet at www.arcadiapublishing.com

I would like to dedicate this book to all of the pioneers who endured the wild of North Texas to build a community that has grown into the wonderful town of Pilot Point. I also especially want to dedicate it to Clifton Irick, former mayor and businessman in Pilot Point for 70 years. By growing up in Pilot Point, through the years, Clifton has acquired an extensive number of photographs and history. Without the inspiration and help of Clifton Irick, none of this would have been possible.

CONTENTS

ACKNOWLEDGMENTS

The majority of the images in this book are from the collection of Clifton Irick and unless otherwise noted were provided by him for publication. Elwood Branum, Calvary Baptist Church, Ruby Ray, Eli Sledge, Weldon Bruce, the late Kenneth Yarbrough, Ronnie Foutch, Vera Jo Cordell, the *Pilot Point Post Signal*, Bob Albrecht–Pilot Point Opera House, Dorothy Yarbrough, Bob Brown, and Dwaine Lawson provided additional images. Special thanks to J. C. Hughes, Randy Hosea, Mario Cisneros, and the City of Pilot Point for their cooperation in obtaining information and images. Photographs and documents from the author's collection are also included.

I would also like to say special thanks to Elwood Branum, who spent many hours scanning the images and also helped by proofreading the copy for historical accuracy. I can't say enough about how he helped me get past the obstacles. Thank you also to Nadene Irick, who allowed me and Clifton to spread old photographs all over the living room floor. Thank you to my wife, Carolyn, who tried to not be bothered by the big mess in my home office. The most important thank-you goes to God, who led me to Pilot Point.

INTRODUCTION

In the early part of the 1800s, the land where the city of Pilot Point is situated and the surrounding area was occupied entirely by tribes of the Caddodochan Confederacy. The Ouchitas had been in the upper Trinity Valley for over 300 years. Beginning in about 1830, other tribes came into this area, including the Ionies, the Keechies, and the Caddos. They came because the hunting and fishing were great in the black land prairie that was on the border of the great cross-timbers woodland. The prairie was abundant with grasses and other plants, and the wooded sections grew nuts and many kinds of wild fruits. This provided a natural habitat for game animals and birds. The area also had a number of streams and springs of clear fresh water.

Charles M. Smith came to Texas in 1836 and was granted a parcel of land in the north Trinity Valley, under the colonization laws of the government of Mexico. Smith never lived to settle in the area, but the Republic of Texas assigned his wife, Sophia Smith, the rights to this grant in 1845. In 1843, the Republic of Texas opened the "Preston Road," which allowed settlers access to this area, and the family farmers, buffalo hunters, and cattle ranchers soon followed. By 1845, several large family farms were established and log cabins were built out of what material was available. In 1853, D. W. Light founded a large cattle ranch in the area with its famous "53" brand, signifying the year of its beginning. Sophia Smith remarried to James Pierson, who in 1853 formulated the plan to lay out a town on the Shoenee Trail. The trail, which was a supply route for the frontier Native American forts, ran just to the west of the present-day Pilot Point Square. The wagon masters and pilots of these supply trains used the highest point in the area, which was marked with a large stand of cottonwood trees, as a reference point on the trail to locate the best crossings for the river. This little hill, which was clearly visible for some miles around, became known as the pilot's point. It also had an ideal campground just to the north, which was known as Dripping Springs because of the constant supply of freshwater that dripped from the rock outcropping. This campground and the grove of trees to the south had also been widely used by the Native Americans, who told the early settlers the "Big Winds" (tornadoes) had never hit the trees growing on the hill. Settlers began to take their advice and began building around the grove of trees.

On Christmas day in 1853, a surveyor named G. W. Newcome from Kentucky Town in Grayson County, together with James Pierson, laid out the plat for the town of Pilot Point. It is said that they surveyed the streets to the south of the square in the morning and then they took a break for an afternoon of Christmas celebration. When they resumed the surveying in the late afternoon, they were somewhat less than sober, and consequently the streets to the north of the square are all crooked. The survey was certified anyway, and on February 11, 1854, it was made official. The Newcome survey was recorded in the records of Denton County on June 28, 1854. Shortly after, Pierson began selling lots in the new town. One of his first customers was Dr. R. W. Eddleman and his wife, Alvina, who moved to the area from Missouri in 1852 and lived in a log cabin west of town. Dr. Eddleman built the Star Drug Store on the north side of the newly formed square, near the west end, and his sister's husband, Maj. James D. Walcott, purchased the land on the east end of the north side of the square. Major Walcott built a log house on the property and opened the first general merchandise store on the corner lot in late 1854. Abigail Linch pitched a tent on the present site on the Pilot Point City Hall and opened a hotel, and thus commerce was in full swing in the city. Early on, it became necessary to provide a mill for grinding corn and wheat to help feed the growing population. J. D. Rankin had built a mill west of town, which was purchased by J. C. Thomas and Jim Graham and moved one block south of the square. Jefferson Elmore and "Uncle" Nick Wilson later bought the gristmill and built their homes across from it where the water tower now stands. The mill consisted of a large tread wheel for oxen to walk on. When the oxen walked on the wheel, it moved around and the power was transferred to the millstones. The circular stones were about 40 inches in diameter and 8 inches thick. The grain fed into a hopper was then ground into a meal or flour. The original burrstones from this mill are imbedded in the asphalt at the crosswalk on Washington and Liberty Streets and may be seen today.

In 1856, Alvina Eddleman gave birth to the first child born in the new settlement, L. Z. Eddleman. James Pierson died in 1856, and his only child, Margaret Pierson, inherited the remaining property. Also in 1856, Alphius Knight, a New Yorker, built a frame schoolhouse on the northwest corner of Liberty and Hill Streets. Yankee Knight's school, as it was called, was a "subscription school" as there were no free schools at this time. The First Baptist Church was also organized in 1856 by Elder Asa Davis, Dr. J. T. Harris, and S. D. Sneed and was pastored by Rev. J. R. Masters. In 1858, the Texas Legislature passed an act allowing the incorporation of Pilot Point; it was, however, not incorporated until 1866. Gradually, because of the delightful climate and productive soil, the forests were cleared, crops were planted, and buildings were erected. Here and there, patches of corn and cotton could be seen. Businesses were built, and the town became active and prosperous.

Beginning in the mid-19th century, downtown Pilot Point served as an important commercial center in an area based largely on an agricultural economy. The Pilot Point commercial district includes historic commercial properties and buildings that retain architectural integrity, reflecting the historic character of the Pilot Point community. The overall appearance of the square has changed very little. In 2002, Pilot Point became a Texas Main Street Community, and this created a desire to bring new life to the downtown area. In 2007, the Pilot Point Commercial District was designated a National Historic District by the U.S. National Parks Service and was listed in the National Register of Historic Places.

One

1850s through 1890s

Dr. R. W. Eddleman came to Pilot Point in 1852 with his mother, Cynthia, and wife, Alvina. He built this cabin on the bluff overlooking the Trinity River. This photograph from 1875 shows the Eddleman log house, which in the 1880s was expanded into a Victorian home. The home and the cabin still stand, along with the old barn that dates to the Civil War. Dr. R. W. Eddleman traveled by wagon from Missouri to Texas in 1852. Maj. James Walcott, his brother-in-law, came with him, as did his mother and sisters. When the town square lots were available, they were among the first to build businesses there. Dr. Eddleman opened a drugstore and Major Walcott a general store. (Author's collection.)

The Pilot Point Masonic Lodge was organized on June 18, 1861, and was chartered as No. 270 the following year. Work on this building began in 1870, and 10 months later, it was finished. The building was constructed with huge oak sills hewn square by hand with a broad ax. The finished lumber was hauled from Jefferson, Texas, by oxen. It served as a Sunday meeting place for several early churches. The building was used until 1985, when it was demolished.

Dr. R. W. Eddleman and his wife, Alvina, came to Pilot Point by wagon from Missouri in 1852. When the town of Pilot Point was laid out in 1854, he purchased a lot on the north side and built the Star Drug Store, a log building. The building in this image replaced the log structure in 1872 when bricks became available for building in Pilot Point. Dr. and Mrs. Eddleman are shown here in the doorway of their new building in 1872.

The Texas Historical Commission placed a historical marker on the town square of Pilot Point in 1978. The marker reads in part, "Attracted by fertile land and abundant water, pioneers began to settle at this site . . . in the late 1840s. The village, first known as Pilot's Point, was named for a high point of timber that served travelers as a landmark. Pilot Point was also a stop on the Butterfield Stage route. A town site was platted in 1854 on land originally granted to Charles Smith. Dr. R. W. Eddleman of Missouri . . . opened a drug store. James D. Walcott ran the earliest general store and became the first postmaster in 1855. Alphius Knight, a settler from New York, built the first school." (Courtesy of *Pilot Point Post Signal*.)

The Church of Christ congregation purchased the land and built this structure on October 20, 1874. J. N. Gist and J. C. Blake, deacons of the church, bought the land on Jefferson Street from George W. Merchant for $100. The building was finished in 1875. Much of the lumber for the framework was cut locally, and the bark can still be seen on the split logs that make up the roof. The 1875 congregation numbered 75 with meetings on Sunday and Thursday night. The building, which has a state historical marker, is still used today.

The Pilot Point Baptist Church was organized in 1856. It was the second Baptist church established in Denton County, the first being Lonesome Dove Church in the southern part of the county. The first church building was destroyed in a storm in early 1879, and the church building pictured was built later that same year. Reverends Asa Davis, T. J. Harris, and S. D. H. Steed were the early pastors.

When John Hundley arrived in Pilot Point in 1870, he noted that the clay along the river was suitable for brick making, which was his trade. The next year, he built a brick kiln and set about to convince merchants to replace their wooden buildings with brick ones. This photograph of the north side of the town square is from 1872 and shows the first brick building constructed in Denton County. A general store on the lower floor and the Odd Fellows Lodge Hall on the upper level occupied the two-story building on the left end. The Star Drug Store is the next building to the right, followed by several wooden buildings.

Pilot Point was growing fast in the 1870s, as evidenced by this photograph from that time. The streets were crowded with horses and buggies as the farmers converged on the town square to sell their produce and buy supplies. This is a view of Main Street looking east from the square. The north side is shown on the left and the east side on the right.

The Pilot Point Seminary, which became Franklin College, the largest university in North Texas in the 19th century, was established in 1872. This building, a large three-story frame structure, was built from lumber hauled by oxen from East Texas. The belfry housed a bell that was purchased from a steamboat on the Red River. When the college first opened in September 1872, more than 300 students attended classes. The first headmaster was J. C. Newberry. It was chartered in 1892 as Franklin College when Dr. M. B. Franklin purchased it. It closed in 1900 when free public education came into being.

Pilot Point Seminary was known throughout the area for its fine arts and literature departments. It conferred Bachelor of Arts and Bachelor of Science degrees. It also granted the "Mistress of English Literature" degree to young ladies who had not completed the courses in Greek, Latin, and mathematics required for an advanced degree. The announcement shown here is from 1882. (Author's collection.)

14

Maj. James D. Walcott was one of the first merchants on the town square in 1854 when he opened his general store on the north side. The young men and ladies in this picture are his children, who were among the first pioneer children born in the new settlement. They are pictured here with Mattie on the left and Loren on the right; Martha Walcott is in the center. Standing in the back are Arthur (left) and Everett (right). (Author's collection.)

The Texas and Pacific Railroad, which had reached Sherman, Texas, in the early 1870s, decided to extend the line on to Fort Worth. The surveying was done in 1875. The grading of the roadbed and the laying of track began immediately. This wooden depot was built just in time for the first train, which arrived in the fall of 1880. A few years later, the Missouri, Kansas, and Texas Railroad leased a right-of-way, giving Pilot Point service from two railroad lines.

15

East Side Sq. Pilot Point- Tex - Nov. 1884.

The east side of the town square is shown in this photograph from November 1884. The wagons in the center of the picture contain 250 bales of cotton that were being delivered to the cotton gin for processing. In the background are the Masonic Lodge Hall in the center left and the new First Methodist church on the right. It was about this time that the brick buildings began replacing the earlier wooden ones. Several of the earlier wooden buildings can be seen on the left and also on the extreme right.

The first bank in Pilot Point opened on January 1, 1884, and was called Pilot Point Bank. Alexander Hamilton Gee was cashier and manager, with J. M. Weeks as president and J. A. L. McFarland as assistant cashier. By 1887, the bank had a capital of $25,000. In 1892, the capital was increased to $60,000 and Gee became president. The bank received a federal charter, and the name was changed to Pilot Point National Bank. This image, of the inside of the original location, shows Gee on the left and Weeks on the right.

In 1892, the Pilot Point National Bank built a new stone building on the northeast corner of the town square. The bank had been very successful under the leadership of Alexander Gee, and this new building reflected that success. In 1974, when the bank moved to a new location, this building was given to the City of Pilot Point and was used as city hall until 2000. At that time, it was renovated and now is the police department.

Several small newspapers sprang up in Pilot Point during the 1870s, but none lasted very long until 1878, when the *Pilot Point Post* began publishing. Founded by J. T. Jones (below) and David J. Moffitt (left), the newspaper began publishing on August 31, 1878, and has been published continuously ever since, making it the oldest continuously published publication in North Texas. The *Post* merged with the *Pilot Point Mirror* and then later with the *Pilot Point Signal*. Today it is the *Pilot Point Post Signal*.

William Story McShan built the Peters Boarding House in 1879. It remained a private home for many years but in the 1920s became a boardinghouse for maiden schoolteachers. The Peters Boarding House was remembered by many as the home of a very loud parrot that lived on the porch. The parrot would shout at passersby and confuse visitors.

In the 1870s, east of the square, Henery Selz built the first cotton gin to accommodate the local farmers in the area. It later burned and was rebuilt in 1882 north of the square by Selz and his new partner, J. P. Cooper. This new gin, known as the Cooper-Selz Gin, was the largest cotton gin west of the Mississippi River. The gin continued to operate until late in the 20th century, although it changed owners several times. This picture from 1906 shows the vast stores of cotton awaiting rail shipment to market.

The First Methodist Church was established in 1856 by circuit-riding minister William E. Bates of Gainesville, Texas. For several years, they met in various log cabins, but in November 1870, they began meeting in the new Masonic Lodge. The new lodge building was a joint project for the Masons and the Methodists, serving as a meeting hall and a church. In 1883, the Methodists decided to build this brick structure on the corner next to the lodge building. They gave their part of the building and half of the lot in exchange for the adjoining lot to the south. The new Methodist church was a tall, red-brick structure with a bell tower. Steep steps led to the main entrance, and worshippers could also enter through a door in the bell tower. The pulpit in the sanctuary was high above the audience and the ceiling was lofty. Foundation problems caused this building to be torn down in 1910 and replaced.

This building was originally the local canning factory. Area farmers sold their produce to be processed for canning. Built in 1882 on land adjoining the railroad track, the factory produced large amounts of corn and pears and lesser amounts of local vegetables. The business was a boon to local farmers until the 1890s, when factories began to can food more efficiently. In 1892, the factory was closed and then reopened as the Pilot Point Power and Ice Company, furnishing electric power to the town square and local residents. A well was drilled to provide water for the manufacture of ice. In 2006, the water from this well was still being used in the Pilot Point city water system.

One of the most important businesses in town in the 1880s was the wagon yard, shown here in 1888. Just north of the town square on Washington Street, all types of wagons and farm implements were sold. Advertising for Olds, Studebaker, and Weber wagons can be seen on the building, as well as signs for John Deere and Aultman-Taylor farming equipment. The impressive size of this building and the location on the main road into town let visitors know that they were entering a major commercial center in North Texas.

Pictured here is a view from the square, looking northwest, taken about 1892. Noticeably missing from the corner is the Farmer's and Merchant's Bank building, which was not built until 1899. The house on the corner was the private home of the Decker family. Dallas County sheriff Bill Decker was born in this house. Decker was sheriff in Dallas in 1963 during the Kennedy assassination. The two-story building on the north corner, built in 1872, is the oldest brick building in Denton County.

Dr. R. W. Eddleman, whose cabin appears on page 9, expanded his home in 1872. He had lumber brought from East Texas to enclose his original cabin and build the farmhouse shown here. The new home followed the original roof design of the cabin, as can be seen by comparing the two images. In the early 1890s, the house was once again renovated, and a second floor with wraparound porches was added. The house still stands today, although it is in need of repair.

M. M. Marable's Photography Studio made most of the early photographs in Pilot Point. Located on the west side of the square in the 1880s, Marable's images are the only records of early Pilot Point citizens. The girl in the photograph is Mary Emberson from the Emberson Ranch, a large cattle business east of town in the 1880s and 1890s. The photograph of the young man was found in the Emberson family estate, but his identity is unknown. These two images are representative of Marable's work.

In the 1880s, there were nine saloons on the town square, the city was unincorporated, and the law of the West prevailed. The Midway Saloon was one of the most famous located on Main Street. It was not unusual for gunfights to break out at any time. When the trail cowboys rode into town, it was especially dangerous, as they had not usually seen a saloon in many weeks. Houser's Saloon located on the south side of the square was also a popular hangout for gunfighters and cowboys. The last gunfight on the streets of Pilot Point occurred in 1905 in front of the Midway Saloon. The saloons continued to operate on the square until Prohibition made their business illegal in 1918.

This photograph of the cowboys was taken in 1895 just south of the town square. Pilot Point was on the trails going to the northern markets and was frequently visited by unruly trail cowboys. In this photograph, traveling peddlers are seen hawking their wares to the crowd. Behind the building on the right, the tall grain storage bins of the Pilot Point Roller Mill can be seen.

G. B. Moffitt opened his jewelry store on the west side of the square in 1894. He began by selling and repairing watches but soon expanded into ladies' jewelry and millinery. Although his building was only 12.5 feet wide, it was crammed wall to wall with items that enticed the ladies to spend their husbands' money.

From this view looking west, the Pilot Point Roller Mill is shown in the foreground with its large grain storage bins. The mill was one of the first businesses in Pilot Point, having been founded by Jefferson Elmore and Nick Wilson in 1857. A large tread wheel on which oxen walked powered the original mill. When the oxen walked on the wheel, the power was transferred to the 40-inch millstones that ground the flour. This photograph from 1896 also shows some of the large homes that were located on Hill Street west of the railroad tracks. At this time, Hill Street was considered the "silk stocking row," with most of the town's merchants building their homes there.

This image of the interior of the mill shows the large hoppers and machinery used to manufacture the commercial flour made here. The relaxed worker on the left is Orley Sipes; the center figure is Homer Stephens. The man on the right is unidentified. (Author's collection.)

The machinery in the roller mill can be seen in this photograph from 1910. Bags of flour are shown in the foreground. Pilot Point Roller Mill made two different brands of flour.

Study This Book Carefully

And Bring Your Grain to Us

PILOT POINT ROLLER MILL CO

ROYAL ARCH

HIGH PATENT

PILOT POINT, TEX.

ROYAL ARCH

HIGHEST MARKET PRICE PAID FOR ALL GRAIN

We Make and Sell the Highest Grade Flour for the Least Money

ALL FLOUR GUARANTEED

Pilot Point Roller Mill Co.

The Pilot Point Roller Mill Company produced two grades of flour—a commercial grade called Royal Arch and an extra-fancy grade known as Gold Crown. This daily business calendar from 1895 was given to farmers and merchants in the area. It advertises "highest prices paid for grain" and "highest quality flour." (Author's collection.)

Panoramic views of towns gained popularity in the 1880s, and Pilot Point was no exception to this new technology. This image looks to the east to highlight the skyline of the growing city. Here in the late 1890s, most of the landmark buildings can be seen in this photograph. On the center left is the First Baptist Church, built in 1879. In the center left background is the Masonic

Lodge Hall built in 1870, and the Methodist church with its tall steeple is to the right of the lodge. The Pilot Point School, a two-story wood-framed building constructed in 1898, is shown on the far right.

In 1894, the school district was established in Pilot Point. New laws in the state of Texas mandated free public education, and a frame building was built. The first school board members were George Light, W. B. McShan, J. R. Jones, W. B. Montgomery, Henery Selz, and F. S. Wilson. A 50¢ tax was levied to support the construction of a new stone and brick school building in 1898. Shown in these school pictures from 1895 and 1896 are students from grades 1 through 12. Prof. Rufus Strawn, the first superintendent, is on the far right in the top photograph.

By 1895, Pilot Point had established a Trade Day, the second Monday of each month. The photograph shown here depicts a typical Trade Day from about 1905. Looking southeast from the town square, the Cloer Hotel is visible as the two-story structure. Behind the hotel is the steeple of the 1884 Methodist church. On the right is the south side of the square with the steeple of the Presbyterian church in the background.

The Pilot Point Cotton Seed Oil Mill was built to use the by-products of the ginning process and turn it into cottonseed oil, which was in great demand at that time. The oil mill continued to operate until 1930, when the cotton market hit rock bottom. The gin continued to process cotton until the 1980s. (Courtesy of the *Pilot Point Post Signal*.)

The Yeary Cottage

Mrs. M. A. Yeary, Prop.

Rates $2.00 Per Day
Good Sample Rooms

Pilot Point, Tex. 9/10/ 1913.

[handwritten letter on Yeary Cottage stationery]

The Yeary Cottage was a hotel for traveling salesmen who visited Pilot Point to sell their wares to the businessmen on the town square. Built in the late 1880s, it featured a large showroom for these drummers to display their goods. Located on North Washington Street just off the square and within a few blocks of the train depot, it was the most popular hotel for salesmen. It continued in operation until 1930, when it caught fire and burned in one of the largest fires in the history of downtown as of that date. The letter shown here on Yeary Cottage stationery is from September 1913, offering to settle a note payment on some property.

Two

1900s through 1920s

The Pilot Point Opera House was built in 1894 on the top of R. T. Evans Hardware on the west side of the town square. The lower floor was originally built in 1889, with the idea of adding a second floor at some future time. The opera house was completed in 1894, and the first production, *Siege of the Alamo*, was performed on October 11 that year. It was directed by John Weldorn and featured the Pilot Point Amateurs. (Author's collection.)

The Pilot Point String Band performed at the opening of the Pilot Point Opera House in 1894. The members are shown in this photograph. It is believed that this picture was posed several years later by a photographer featuring only some of the original members. Music of this type was featured in many early opera houses of this era.

The Farmer's and Merchant's Bank was established in 1899, and a new building was built on the northwest corner of the town square. The Light brothers, D. W. Light Jr. and George Light, who were well-established cattle ranchers in Pilot Point, founded the bank. Their father, D. W. Light Sr., ran the Light Ranch, the old "53" brand, indicating the date of the founding of their ranch. This building is the best example of Richardsonian-Romanesque architecture known to exist in the United States. The second floor of this building was doctors' and dentists' offices.

This view of the north and west corners of the town square is from a postcard folio of Pilot Point sold by J. R. Peel Drug Store about 1905. It shows the new Farmer's and Merchant's Bank building on the corner and the oldest brick building in Denton County on the north corner. At this time, the building was the home to Cosgrove Grocery Store and J. R. Peel Drug Store.

When the town was first laid out in 1854, one immediate need was a cemetery. Some ground was selected north of town, and the first burial was made in 1855. J. E. Hayden was hired to grade the land with mules and a dragstone. The burial ground was originally maintained by the Independent Order of Odd Fellows (IOOF). Responsibility was later transferred to the Masonic Lodge when they expanded the cemetery. The pavilion shown here was built in 1900

The Autry family in Pilot Point produced several blacksmiths near the dawn of the 20th century. This photograph is the blacksmith shop of Johnny Autry located on the corner of East Main Street and North Church Street in Pilot Point. Autry is standing in front of the shop.

This photograph shows the inside of Johnny Autry's blacksmith shop. Taken in about 1910, the picture highlights the tools and equipment used by turn-of-the-century blacksmiths. Note the 400-pound anvil that Johnny is using to make a plowshare in the center of the picture.

By 1905, the town square was a major center of commerce in the North Texas area. This view of the west and north sides shows the activity on a typical Monday Trade Day. In the center is the Farmer's and Merchants Bank. On the left side are R. T. Evans Hardware and Dry Goods Stores. In this photograph, one can see that Pilot Point Town Square was wired for electricity, being one of the first towns in North Texas to receive this benefit.

The first U.S. Post Office was opened in Pilot Point on June 12, 1855, with Maj. James Walcott as postmaster. It was located in his general store. In 1858, the Butterfield Stage Line opened a station on Liberty Street and the post office was moved there to receive the overland mail. The post office was moved several times and by 1905 was located north of the square behind the National Bank building. This photograph depicts some of the postal workers from that time.

Behind the scenes at the Pilot Point Post Office in about 1900, the workers are sorting the mail. The post office later was moved to the west side of the square in the 1940s and then later to the north side in the 1950s. Today it is located three blocks north of the town square. There have been 19 postmasters in Pilot Point in the last 150 years.

This view of the north side of the square is from about 1895. Joe B. Burks is pictured here passing in front of Graves Market. At the far end of the street the decorative front of Devenport's Dry Goods can be seen. Burks was later one of the founders of the Farmer's and Merchant's Bank in 1899.

The Pilot Point School District built a brick school on Prairie Street in 1898. The new school was the pride of the town. Constructed of red bricks, it was home to all grades from 1 to 12. The school only remained for 25 years and was torn down in 1923 to make room for a new, modern school.

This postcard, mailed from Pilot Point on January 21, 1909, shows some of the landmark buildings of the period. The Pilot Point High School is shown in the lower left. The Farmer's and Merchant's Bank is pictured in the lower right. The upper right of the photograph shows the home of Alexander H. Gee, president of the Pilot Point National Bank.

This photograph shows the home of Alexander Gee on East Liberty Street. Gee's home was a showplace in Pilot Point. After building it in the 1890s, Gee lived there until his death in 1929. It remained vacant for a number of years. In 1943, city employees were burning leaves and the fire became out of control. The ensuing grass fire ignited the Gee home, and it was burned to the ground.

The Pilot Point State Bank opened on the west side of the square about 1900. This photograph shows the interior of that building. It was moved to a larger building on the north side in 1915. It continued to operate until the Depression caused many banks to fail in 1930.

The Peters Hardware Store was located on the west side of the town square, as were most businesses appealing to men. The west side was reserved primarily for male-orientated businesses as it was considered unsafe for ladies to cross the main road leading through town. N. M. Peters also operated a boardinghouse south of downtown that was used mainly by female schoolteachers. A close examination of this photograph shows horse collars on the left wall and razor straps hanging on the right wall.

Using the railroad connections, the elite of Pilot Point organized shopping trips to neighboring towns. This photograph from 1918 pictures the Sherman trade excursion gathering on the town square in preparation for the trip. Most of the town's women and children turned out in their Sunday best for these trips. The buildings shown in the background from left to right are Davenport's Variety Store, Pilot Point National Bank, and several other businesses on Main and Jefferson Streets.

The center of the town square offers plenty of parking in this 1905 photograph of the east side of the square. The circle with is hitching fence accommodated over 100 horses at times. Carlton's Furniture and Henderson and Flake Grocery are among the businesses in the background. On the right, the steeple of the Central Christian Church rises in the background.

Local businessmen in Pilot Point celebrated Christmas in 1910 by posing for this photograph. Shown from left to right are (first row, on the floor) Mont Pebley; (second row, with the dog) J. P. "Uncle Polk" Cooper; (third row) Jim Jones, J. B. Clifton, Alexander H. "Sandy" Gee, Henery Selz, W. C. Dowdell, and Pole Webster; (fourth row) S. Newton, Sheriff John Lewis Bates, G. V. Harrison, Rufe Thomas, and W. B. "Kit" Carson. Selz and Cooper owned the cotton gin, Pilot Point's largest industry.

The cook's wagon was often seen on the prairies of North Texas in the 1890s. This photograph from 1897 was taken on a ranch east of Pilot Point. Cattle drives passed this way en route to northern markets.

Modern farming methods came to Pilot Point, as shown in this 1915 photograph. The large cotton-producing fields around the area required farmers to keep abreast of new developments.

Cotton was the largest crop grown in the Pilot Point area in the late 1880s. Almost all of the farmers grew cotton, and many of them helped each other by sharing harvesting equipment and labor. This picture shows farmers working together to bring in a crop of wheat.

In 1905, J. R. Peel Drug Store produced a folio of postcards of local scenes in Pilot Point. This image, from that folio, shows the north and east sides. The Pilot Point National Bank can be recognized in the center with its tall roof. To the north of the bank is the two-story lodge building of the Woodmen of the World. The U.S. Post Office was on the lower floor with the lodge hall upstairs. The buildings on the extreme right on the east side of the square were a saloon and grocery.

On February 3, 1903, Rev. J. P. Roberts purchased the old Franklin College property, which included a large house, and opened Rest Cottage. Originally an orphanage, it gradually became a refuge for "wayward girls." The Rest Cottage facility included a main building with 22 rooms that could accommodate up to 35 girls. The home eventually became known as a home for unwed mothers and was licensed by the Texas Department of Public Welfare to operate as an adoption agency. From 1904 until it closed in 1974, over 7,000 children were born here.

The orphans of Rest Cottage are shown here in this photograph from 1908. The purpose of Rest Cottage was not only to care for the unwed mothers but also to find suitable homes for the babies born there. It had a convalescent ward with a capacity for five mothers and beds for six babies. These were under the direction of an M.D., registered nurse, and assistant nurses.

This bird's-eye view of the town square looking north was taken in 1908. The Farmer's and Merchant's Bank (left) and the Pilot Point National Bank (right) mark the two north corners. The Pilot Point Opera House can be seen on the west side (left), with the Commercial Hotel and Ragland's Drug Store in the foreground.

This 1904 postcard looks south on Church Street. The reason this is called Church Street is obvious, as most of the churches in Pilot Point were built on this street from the beginning. Shown at left is the newly completed (1902) Central Christian Church. The next building is the Masonic Lodge Hall (1870), followed by the Methodist church (1884). In the far distance, the tall steeple of the First Presbyterian Church can be seen.

The Church of the Nazarene was founded in Pilot Point in 1908, the result of the merging of three independent groups already in existence in the United States. The Association of Pentecostal Churches from New England, the Church of the Nazarene from California, and the Holiness Churches of Christ from the South all met in Pilot Point to establish the national Church of the Nazarene. The property of the defunct Franklin College was used as the meeting place, and on October 13, 1908, the groups voted to unite. It was a noteworthy happening when a Southern delegate crossed the platform to hug a Northern delegate "for the first time in a while, it being so soon after the [Civil] war."

Alexander Gee of the Pilot Point National Bank gave the Catholic mission 4 acres of land on the northeast of town and $500 with which to start a church. Plans for a new building were drawn up, and work began on a two-story frame structure 60 feet long, 28 feet wide, and 24 feet high. Both Catholics and members of other local churches worked to build the church. The new church was completed in early 1892 and Father Coffey sang the first high mass on February 9, 1892. The church was dedicated to the honor of St. Thomas Aquinas. The first resident priest was Fr. Hugo Bardenhewer.

G. B. Moffitt was the son of the founder of the *Pilot Point Post* newspaper, but he became a jeweler. Moffitt began his jewelry shop in the 1890s, and by 1908, he had expanded to include ladies millinery. The picture above is from about 1908, and the one below is from the 1890s. Moffitt (on the far right above and below) displays his wares in his building on the west side of the square.

Henderson's Cash Grocery on the east side of the square is shown here in about 1895. Many grocery stores came and went on the east side for a number of years, including David Grocery, Luper's Grocery, Mountain's Market, and Stephens Grocery.

This early grocery store was also on the east side of the town square. This photograph, probably Pole Baxter's grocery, is from about 1909 and shows the simplicity of the marketing from that time. Baxter later became partners with Homer Stephens and formed Baxter and Stephens Grocery, with Stephens buying him out in 1926 to become sole proprietor. Homer Stephens's great-grandchildren still operate Stephens's grocery today.

R. T. Evans Hardware started business on the west side of the square in the early 1890s. This photograph is from that time. Evans was instrumental in helping form the city government when the town was incorporated for the second time in 1906. He was elected as the first mayor of Pilot Point. His hardware business continued until about 1918, when he sold out to N. M. Peters and moved to Vernon, Texas.

From the pages of the 1915 Pilot Point Telephone Book comes this advertisement for R. T. Evans Hardware Store. At one time, the Evans complex of hardware and dry goods stores occupied most of the west side of the square. (Author's collection.)

NORTH TEXAS

TELEPHONE COMPANY

"Look For The Shield"

USE INDEPENDENT SERVICE
FIGHTING
THE TRUST
LOCAL AND LONG DISTANCE

This Company, in connection with other
Companies, is now giving long distance
service to many towns and cities in Texas

PILOT POINT EXCHANGE
DIRECTORY
MAY
1915

The front cover of the 1915 telephone directory for the Pilot Point exchange is shown here. There were well over 100 listings for individuals and businesses. Most of the numbers were three digits, although some were one or two digits. It is interesting to note that the author discovered this phone book in a pile of trash about to be destroyed. (Author's collection.)

The railroad built a new depot in Pilot Point around 1905. This new brick building replaced the old wooden depot from the 1880s. The new depot was located at the end of Depot Street north of the square (now Scott Street). Many passengers boarded here for trips to Denton and Fort Worth. The first automobile in Pilot Point was delivered at this depot in 1905 for Dr. Oliver Clinton Buster.

In 1915, a petition signed by 500,000 schoolchildren asked that Philadelphians send the Liberty Bell to the Panama-Pacific International Exposition in San Francisco. The people agreed, and the bell was transported across the country by rail to San Francisco. This photograph shows the Liberty Bell when it came through Pilot Point in 1915 and stopped at the depot so citizens could see it.

54

The women of Pilot Point organized the 19th Century Club on March 17, 1896. The club became federated with the Texas Women's Clubs in 1898. The women of the club were among the first to lobby for compulsory education. This photograph includes club members from 1905, from left to right: (first row) 1. Snow Flake Chance, 2. Jennie Morton, 3. ? Puckett, 4. ? Ledbetter, 5. Ethel Petty, 6. Gladys Price, 7. Hedda Lou and mother, 8. William Briggs; (second row) 12. Mattie Bradley, 9. May Waddell, 10. Idell Hayden, 11. Isabel Spears, 13. ? Scott, 14. Myrtle Brune, 15. Mary Spears, 16. Lora Marshall, 17. Kate Price, 18. Ruth Sharp, 19. ? Cummins, 20. Norma Joe, 21. ? Waggs, and 22. ? Brown. (Author's collection.)

In 1906, another women's club was formed and then was federated in 1908. Lena Moffitt, Minnie Pickel, Dollie Hayden, Mary Elmore, and others founded the El Progresso club. This yearbook, given to members in September 1908, has the dates, hostesses, and topics of discussion for all the meetings held in 1909. (Author's collection.)

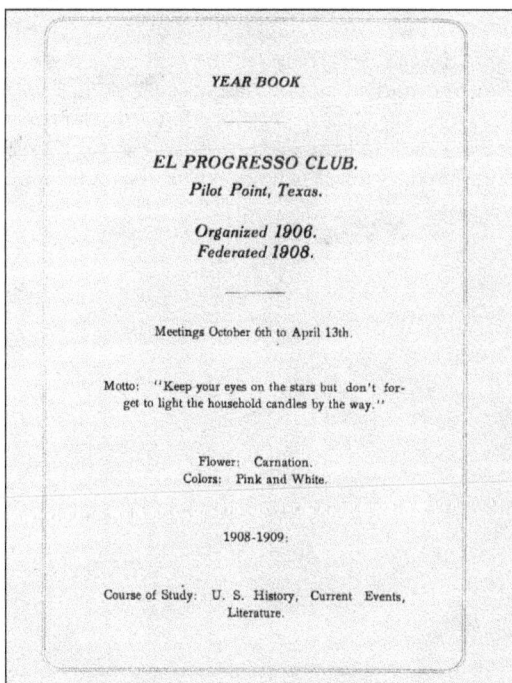

YEAR BOOK

EL PROGRESSO CLUB.
Pilot Point, Texas.

Organized 1906.
Federated 1908.

Meetings October 6th to April 13th.

Motto: "Keep your eyes on the stars but don't forget to light the household candles by the way."

Flower: Carnation.
Colors: Pink and White.

1908-1909:

Course of Study: U. S. History, Current Events, Literature.

PILOT POINT FIRE DEPARTMENT

PHOTO BY
ESCHENBAUM
PILOT POINT

After the city incorporated in 1906, Pilot Point established the Pilot Point Volunteer Fire Department. The first equipment purchases included buckets, rope, an ax, and a ladder. A two-wheel hose reel that was horse drawn was added in 1910. By the 1920s, it was determined that a motorized truck was needed and the American La France pumper shown on the right in this photograph was purchased. A new fire station was also built. The department is pictured here in 1924.

J. Earl Selz, president of the Pilot Point National Bank, stands proudly next to a new fire truck in this photograph from about 1930. Selz was a volunteer fireman, as were most of the businessmen in town. (Author's collection.)

Horses and buggies were commonplace in downtown Pilot Point for many years after automobiles were introduced. This photograph from the late 1920s shows a farm family in town for Saturday Trade Day.

By 1915, the Pilot Point National Bank emerged as the leading financial institution in town under the leadership of Alexander Gee. This photograph of the interior of the bank shows J. A. L. McFarland seated on the left, Gee standing in the center, and J. Earl Selz standing on the right. This building is now the Pilot Point Police Department, and the vault shown here can still be seen today in the police station.

The Pilot Point Bank building was built in 1894, two years after being chartered as a national bank. This image is from about 1915 and shows the Woodmen of the World Lodge Hall on the left behind the bank. The old Pilot Point Ice Company wagon can be seen making a delivery.

Alexander Gee, president of Pilot Point Bank, was a very active community leader. Above, he is shown with the Pilot Point girls' volleyball team in 1902. Gee was the coach of the team, and the bank was the sponsor. The image below depicts the first Boy Scout troop organized in Denton County in 1914. Gee, shown in the back holding the U.S. flag, was the Scout leader. He was a well-respected and generous civic leader until his death in 1929.

Alexander Gee's home was a mansion and showplace in Pilot Point at the turn of the 20th century. Built in the 1890s on 15 acres, it stood alone on the eastern prairie. The three-story classic Victorian house stood at the end of a long tree-lined drive. Gee lived there until his death in 1929. Afterward it was vacant for over 10 years. In 1942, the city was burning leaves in the ditch along the street when the wind caught a spark and ignited the trees. The fire quickly spread to the main house, and it burned to the ground. These two views offer different perspectives of the home, showing the west side in the winter and the south side in the summer.

The Eoanou Market was one of many groceries to operate on the town square at the dawn of the 20th century. There were as many as eight grocery stores and markets downtown at this time. Shown here in 1904, the store was located in a wooden building on the south side of the square. It was shortly after this time that the last of the wooden buildings were replaced with brick.

Cotton was the major crop produced in the Pilot Point area in the late 1800s and early 1900s. The Pilot Point Cotton Oil Mill was built in the 1880s to process oil from the seeds culled by the ginning process. The cotton gin and oil mill both operated until the Depression, when cotton prices went so low that it was no longer feasible for a small farmer to make a living producing it.

P.P.H.S.

The Graduating Class of

Pilot Point High School

requests the honor of your presence at the

Commencement Exercises

Thursday evening at eight-thirty o'clock

May fourteenth

nineteen hundred eight

Weeks' Opera House

CLASS ROLL

Mattie Wells Barnum

Willie Maude Bryant   Minnie Carson

Will J. Hardy   Frank L. Irick

Earl Selz   Stella May Shelton

The Pilot Point High School graduating class of 1908 is shown here on the steps of the brick school, built in 1898 on south Prairie Street. From left to right are (first row) Mattie Wells Barnum, Willie Maude Bryant, Minnie Carson, and Stella Mae Shelton; (second row) J. Earl Selz, Will J. Handy, and Frank L. Irick. The graduation announcement for the 1908 class states that the commencement exercises were held in the Weeks Opera House on May 14, 1908.

J. P. Adcock organized the Central Christian Church in Pilot Point in 1901. He began by holding services in the Masonic Lodge building. In 1902, the congregation began construction on the new church on a lot on the corner of Church and Liberty Streets. The founding members included some of the most prominent families in the town. Green Flake, John Scott, J. P. Conner, and Will Morgen were elders. The Dowdell, Cooper, Evans, Pondrum, and Burks families were some of the founding members.

Many members of the Central Christian Church are shown here in a picture of a church outing in about 1915. Pictured from left to right are Ella Evans, Mary Evelyn Wenckens, ? Myers, Esther Hayden, ? Wenckens, Kathleen Gentles (on mule), Algene Flake, Harold Wenckens, Snow Flake Chance (standing in rear), Jenette Evans, "Uncle" Tom Flake, and Arthur Chance.

According to city documents, in 1915, the Pilot Point Water Department replaced the old wooden water tower, which was built in 1885, with the one shown here. This new water tower, purchased from the Chicago Bridge and Iron Works, stood 125 feet high and had a capacity of 75,000 gallons. The City of Pilot Point signed an agreement in March 1915 to purchase the tower for $4,700. It soon became a town landmark and a favorite camera perch for bird's-eye view photographers. The tower is nicknamed "the Tin Man." (Courtesy of the *Pilot Point Post Signal*.)

The post office moved into the bottom floor of the Woodmen of the World Lodge Hall in the 1890s. By the time of this photograph in 1915, not only were horses and wagons used to deliver the mail, but the new motorized cycles were also being introduced. Postal workers are posed in front of the post office getting ready for a new day of mail delivery.

The Catholic church organized the Pilot Point True-Tone Coronet Band in the early part of the century. Early members included the Strittmatters, Berends, Pelzels, Boerners, and other Catholic families.

This bird's-eye view of Pilot Point was taken from the new water tower soon after it was built. Looking northeast from the tower, the east side of the town square is shown on the extreme left. The livery stable and wagon yard dominate the center of the picture. The First Baptist Church is seen in the center background, and the Central Christian Church is shown on the right.

The Pilot Point Ice Company is pictured in this image making a delivery on Liberty Street. Ice wagons continued to be horse drawn in Pilot Point well past the invention of the automobile.

The Methodist church demolished its red brick structure in 1910 and replaced it with this stately and massive domed house of worship. The new church was built of cream-colored bricks and trimmed in white. Its beautiful stained glass windows and impressive sanctuary were memorable features. Bishop E. E. Hoss dedicated the new church in 1914. The 1910 Methodist church lasted for 74 years until Tuesday, September 11, 1984, when an early-morning fire of undetermined origin destroyed it completely.

The face of the town square was forever changed in 1899 with the addition of the Farmer's and Merchant's Bank building on the northwest corner. This view of the square reflects just how important it was to the commerce of the surrounding area. Shortly after the turn of the century, Pilot Point merchants began offering incentives and giveaways to entice buyers. The first Monday Trade Day eventually gave way to the Saturday Drawings that awarded cash prizes to lucky shoppers. This photograph dates to about 1901.

Many beautiful Victorian homes were built in Pilot Point in the late 1890s. Generally the merchants built these as well as business owners who wanted to be near the downtown area. The photograph above shows the home of Captain Johnson on south Prairie Street. It was later the home of Alfred Coleman. It was torn down in the mid-20th century. The home in the lower image is that of Levi Belew, which was built on south Jefferson Street. Belew owned the grain dealership in Pilot Point, an important business in the early 1900s. Belew was killed in 1923 when the Model T Ford he was driving went out of control on the road to Sanger. The Belew house has been restored and still stands on Jefferson Street in Pilot Point. (Courtesy of the *Pilot Point Post Signal*.)

These two homes were built about the same time in the 1890s. The home pictured above is that of R. T. Evans, who was the first mayor of Pilot Point in 1906 when the city was incorporated. Evans owned and operated the largest hardware store in town. His home on Hill Street still stands as an outstanding example of Victorian architecture in Pilot Point. The photograph below shows the home of the Gracie family, large landowners and cattle ranchers in Pilot Point. It was located on south Washington Street just off the town square. It fell into disrepair in the 1950s and was torn down in 1964 to make way for a new Pilot Point National Bank building on the property. (Courtesy of the *Pilot Point Post Signal*.)

Rev. James Pickney Roberts and his wife, Minnie Roberts, opened an orphanage and home for unwed mothers in Pilot Point in 1904 (see page 38). The Rest Cottage began as a rescue ministry to "wayward girls" but evolved into a completely self-sustaining home for the mothers and adoption agency for the children. (Author's collection.)

When Rev. J. P. Roberts died in 1937, his brother, Rev. John Roberts, assumed the leadership role for Rest Cottage. The main building can be seen in the background as John Roberts poses on the walkway. John Roberts retired from Rest Cottage in 1955, and his son, Rev. Geren Roberts, took over the reins until it closed in 1974.

Rest Cottage covered 31 acres of ground and was almost entirely self-sufficient, with the farm being worked by the girls. It had a garden, an orchard, a vineyard, a berry patch, and chicken house. The dairy and beef cattle, as well as the horses, lived in the barn shown above. Connected to the main property was an additional 41 acres of pasture for the cows and sheep. Nine other buildings dotted the compound, including the superintendent's home, nurses' cottage, cannery, fruit house, dining room, and laundry (shown below).

Panoramic photographs were all the rage in the early 20th century. Many photographers traveled from town to town taking and selling these types of views. This one picture shows almost the entire Pilot Point Town Square. The west side is above on the left with the old opera house and Evans Hardware. The Farmer's and Merchant's Bank stands on the northwest corner as a landmark

building. To the right of the bank is the north side beginning on the left with the IOOF Lodge Hall followed by the First State Bank. Right of the center of this panorama (below) is the Pilot Point National Bank on the northeast corner. The east side is pictured below on the far right. Everyone in town who owned an automobile came to the town square for this photograph in 1920.

When the United States went to war in 1917, many young men in Pilot Point volunteered. This 1917 image shows several boys in their uniforms holding a flag and ready to go "over there." They are assembled with friends and family on the north steps of the Central Christian Church. (Author's collection.)

Calvary Baptist Church was organized on October 15, 1907, after a group of members left the First Baptist Church. Dr. W. C. Lattimore delivered the first sermon and the charge to the church. The building shown in this photograph was built in 1910. In 1921, the church purchased the adjoining property that had a four-room house used for Sunday school. This 1924 image shows the beautiful windows in the church. This building caught fire and burned in October 1959. This photograph of the congregation is from 1924. The minister, Brother Griffith, is in the second row standing third from left. (Courtesy of Calvary Baptist Church.)

76

The girls of Pilot Point High School were in style in the Roaring Twenties with their flapper dresses and bobbed hair. This photograph, taken in front of the school in about 1927, includes, from left to right, Misses Hoyle, Burks, Slaton, McMahon, Kibler, and Bennett.

In 1923, it was decided that the old school building from 1896 was no longer large enough for the growing population of schoolchildren. The old school was demolished, and a new school was built at a cost of $50,000. During construction, classes were held at various churches around town. The school, which faced Prairie Street to the front, White Street to the south, and Grove Street to the north, was opened for classes in 1924.

A parade commemorating the German Catholic settlement in Pilot Point is shown here. The German and Czech Catholics settled here in the 1890s. This image is from about 1928.

The Depression caused many banks to fail and close in 1930. The Farmer's and Merchant's Bank closed its doors during this time and merged its assets with the Pilot Point National Bank.

Three

1930S THROUGH 1940S

The 1930s brought Depression to most of the economy in the United States, but it brought a new prosperity to Pilot Point when oil was discovered on the Jacobs farm. The *Post-Signal* headline read, "$100,000 Changes Hands in Three Days." The well, Jacob's No. 2, had hit it big. Subsequently, a gasoline refinery was built in Pilot Point, producing road oil, kerosene, and two grades of Point Brand gasoline. The discovery of the East Texas oil field a few years later left the oil industry in Pilot Point virtually abandoned.

City Supply and Service Station on Main Street was one of the first stations in Pilot Point. This photograph (above), from about 1926, shows the very earliest style of pumps. This station changed hands several times before it became the home to Massey Ford Company in the mid-1950s. The picture below shows the same building modernized in 1935 as a new Texaco station. The new style of glass-domed gasoline pumps have replaced the old type. The Ford logo indicates that this station was an official Ford repair center. The dealership followed a few years later.

The first Monday Trade Day of the early 1900s evolved into a Trade Day every Saturday from the early 1930s until the 1960s. This photograph from about 1935 shows just how crowded the town square was on a typical Saturday. The east side is in the background with its grocery, dry goods, drug, and hardware stores. All of the businesses on the town square sponsored a drawing for cash prizes every week. Customers could register at any store when they shopped, and their name went into the drawing bin. The usual prize in the 1930s was $10. As the years went by, the payoffs got larger. It was said that on Saturday, in order to step onto the sidewalk, you had to wait for someone else to step off. (Below Author's collection.)

THIS FIRM

IS A CONTRIBUTOR

to the

PILOT POINT

SATURDAY

DRAWING

HELD IN APPRECIATION
OF YOUR PATRONAGE

Your Certificates Honored Here.

Carriers on foot made mail delivery in the city in the 1930s. Rural mail delivery, however, still used horses and wagons until well into the 1940s, as the rural roads were not made for automobile traffic. This is a RFD mail carrier from the 1930s.

H. M. Russell opened a large dry goods store on the south side of the square in 1922. He later sold that store and moved his business to Denton, Texas, where he established Russell's Department Store. He continued to live in Pilot Point until his death. This is a photograph of his home on Hill Street, the silk stocking row popular with merchants in the early days.

Pilot Point fourth-grade schoolchildren posed for this class picture in 1930. The young boy seated second from left in the first row is Clifton Irick, who would later become mayor of Pilot Point as well as a successful business leader.

The community of Friendship located just south of Pilot Point had a one-room school. This class picture from Friendship School is from 1937. In the 1940s, Friendship School was closed and the students were merged with the Pilot Point Independent School District.

Mrs. Copenhaver's Necessity Shop was located on various sides of the square during its 30 or so years of operation. Shown above is Allie Copenhaver on the left and an assistant on the right. In this charming building on the south end of the east side, one could purchase any number of lovely items. Fine white porcelain cups and saucers, bolts of material, sewing notions, nylons, and candies were among the offerings of her shop. The image below shows the outside of the building. Both images are from about 1935.

The southeast corner of the town square is pictured in 1935. On the left is the Pickel and Company Hardware and Furniture Store. Keith Cash Store is in the center. On the south side of Liberty Street on the right is the Cloer Café and Hotel. The two-story hotel was a favorite with commercial travelers who did business on the Pilot Point Square. Silent movies were sometimes shown in the lobby to help draw crowds for drummers to feature their wares.

The west side of the square was home to the U.S. Post Office in the 1930s. On the left is one of the many cafés on the square. On the far left, a portion of the movie theater is visible. The theater was opened in the early 1930s.

The home of T. C. Peters on East Main Street is pictured in this 1930s photograph. Peters built this house in the 1890s when he was the headmaster of Franklin College.

Ruell J. Beck began in the undertaking business at Gray's Furniture and Undertaking in the 1920s. In the mid-1930s, he opened a funeral and undertaking business on Washington Street next to the Farmer's and Merchant's Bank. This photograph shows his building as well as his new hearse.

The Pilot Point Future Farmers of America are shown on the steps of the school in 1937. From left to right are (first row) John B. Alexander, W. N. Booe, Frank Rollins, and Billy Joe Wright; (second row) J. D. Bobble, Robert Taylor, Wendell Osburn, Billy A. Branum, Joe Schindler, Wayne Beatty, Charles Lee Salen, Junior Hammons, Garvin Buell, Francis Pendleton; (third row) Charles O'Dell, Weldon Morrow, Junior Tomberlin, Fenton Bellar, D'Troy Ford, Ray Pedigo, Hershel Gary, Willis Brooks, and D. K. Hoyle, instructor; (fourth row) Oscar Gene Sitzs, Billy Jacobs, Glen Wayne Belcher, John Kenneth Shelton, George Cole, Huston Clark, Ben Jezek, and Billy J. Brown. (Courtesy of Ronnie Foutch.)

The First Assembly of God Church in Pilot Point was formed on August 24, 1924, when an earlier church was reorganized. This photograph of the congregation was taken in 1939. Pastor Martin Tell is shown on the right in the double-breasted suit. (Courtesy of the *Pilot Point Post Signal*.)

In 1943, this aerial view of Pilot Point was taken. The town square can be seen in the lower left corner. The churches of Church Street are across the middle of the picture. And the three-story school is on the right. In the far center background, the buildings of Rest Cottage can be seen.

A wagon rolls past in this photograph of a Harvest Festival at the St. Thomas Aquinas Catholic Church in the 1940s.

The steps of Pilot Point High School were always a popular place to pose for photographs. These girls of the 1930s are just hanging around, probably looking for boys.

Will Geartin (front, second from left) is shown celebrating with his family and other members of the County Line Baptist Church in this late-1930s photograph. Barbeques, church socials, and picnics occupied the free time of Pilot Point citizens during the Great Depression. The County Line Baptist Church is the oldest black church in Denton County, established in 1863. It was recognized with a historical marker by the State of Texas in 2007. (Author's collection.)

About 1944, the old school for African American students burned to the ground. This building was brought in to Pilot Point and opened as the new black school. The building had previously been the Emberson Chapel School, which had closed when it merged with the Pilot Point School in 1940. This was the first Pilot Point school building to have a lunchroom in the building.

Downtown was a busy place during the war years in Pilot Point. This picture of the east side of the square depicts a parade, possibly a high school homecoming, as the streets are lined with onlookers. At the south end of the east side is Branum's Dry Goods.

Chester Cloer, son of the operators of the old Cloer Hotel and Café, opened a shoe store on the south side of the square in the 1940s. Men's accessories such as hats, belts, and ties could also be purchased. Cloer, a bachelor, lived in the rear of the store with his many cats.

Pilot Point High School students are shown in this photograph of the class of 1941. As was usual with class pictures from this time, students are posed on the front steps of the school. (Courtesy of Dwaine Lawson.)

The Cassity-Wilson Drug Store on the north side of the square was a popular hangout for teenagers in the 1940s. The store's soda fountain and comic-book rack attracted the local boys and girls. Standing in front of the drugstore are, from left to right, Clem Dunn Jr., Donald Hall, Joe Tomberlin, Martha Sullivan, and her unidentified friend from Dallas. (Author's collection.)

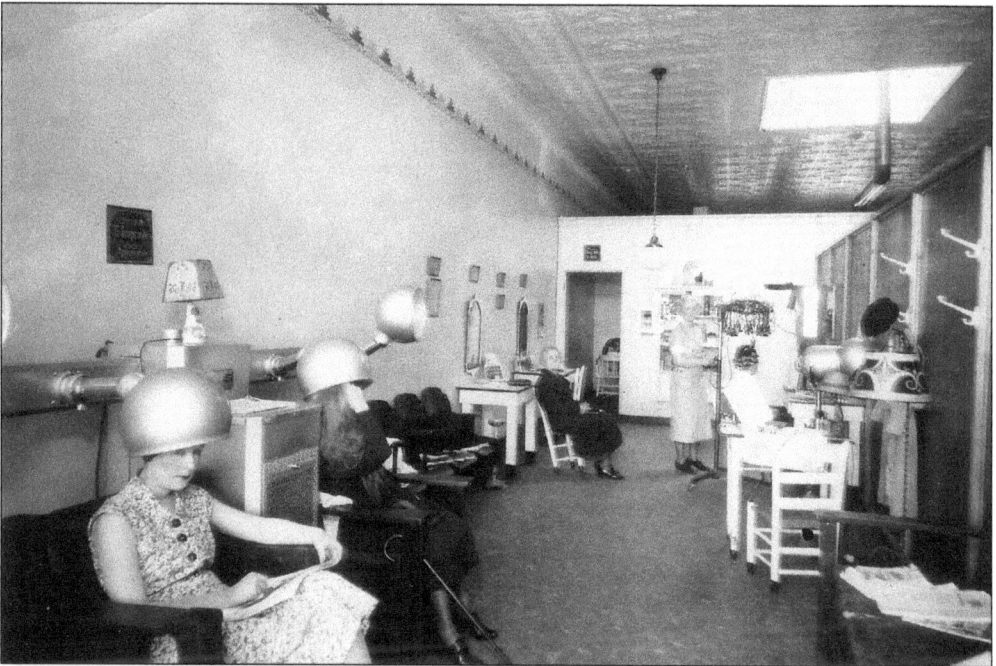

Just east of the drugstore on the north side of the square was Erma Price's Beauty Shop. The 25-foot building was divided into two 12-foot sections with the beauty shop on one side and Luther Price's Barber Shop next door. This image from about 1948 shows Erma Price standing (in uniform) and her mother, Mrs. J. A. Rhodes, seated in the chair behind her. (Author's collection.)

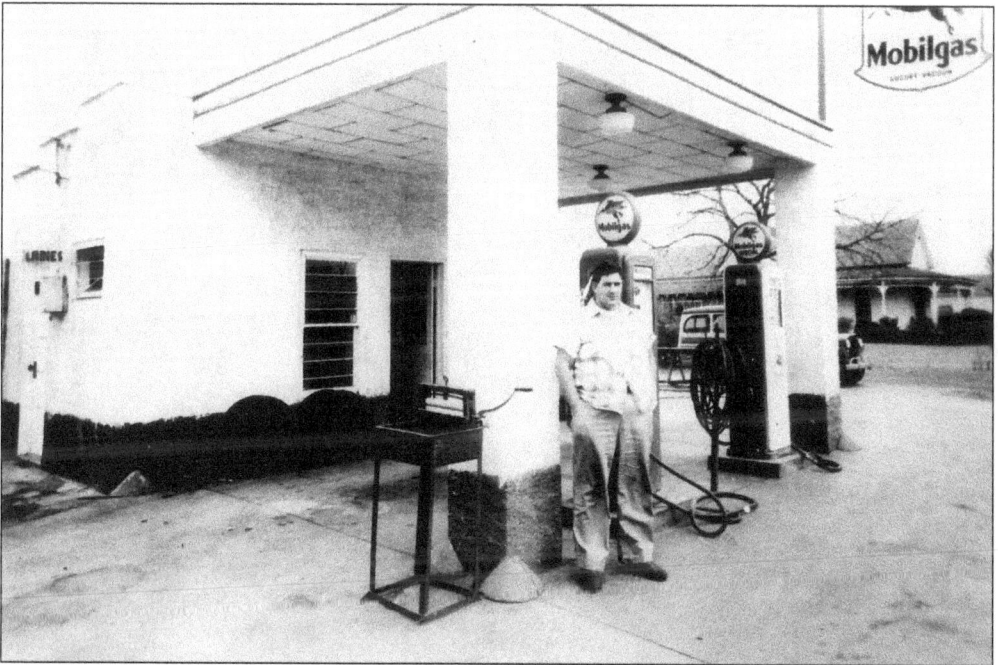

Wayne "Sharkey" Ray purchased the Magnolia Gas Station on Liberty Street from Jim Richardson in the 1940s. Ray is shown here in his new modern Mobilgas Station about 1949. (Courtesy of Ruby Ray.)

Clifton and Nadene Irick had a dream of owning a business on the square. Buildings on the square were rented whenever they became available. While Clifton was away during World War II, Nadene worked to pay rent on an empty store so they could keep the lease on it. They opened White's Auto Store on the south side in 1946. The interior shown here is filled with postwar merchandise in this 1948 photograph. Standing in the store are, from left to right, D'Troy Ford, ? Williams, Will Raney, and Clifton Irick.

When Ruell Beck moved his undertaking business to a new building in the 1940s, he also bought a new, modern hearse. Beck is shown here on the right with his assistant, Maurice Richards, on the left.

Pilot Point volunteer firemen responded to this fire at the home of Hub Henderson in the late 1940s. Standing on the ladder is Billy Bridges, and holding the ladder is Omar Jones. On the far right is Buster Wood. The house was saved, but the roadster was a total loss.

In 1948, the Pilot Point School District built a lunchroom for the school on property across the street. For the first time, the school was able to offer hot lunches to the students, at a site near the school. Previously lunches were served at the community building.

Pilot Point celebrated everything with a parade in the 1940s and 1950s. This parade was in about 1940. The usual celebrations were high school football homecomings or holidays. The fire trucks in the parade date from the 1920s. In the upper left corner, the two-story Cloer Hotel can be seen.

William Hilz opened the City Machine Shop in the 1920s as a combination service station and convenience store, offering automobile service, gasoline, cigars, hardware, and various drinks and snacks. Billy Hilz Jr. and George Hilz are pictured here in the 1940s with the new tow truck for road service. The phone number on the side of the truck is No. 105.

Four

1950s and Beyond

The east side of the town square is the background for this homecoming parade in 1950. The buildings in the background are, from left to right, the Woodmen of the World Lodge Hall (two-story building), Pilot Point National Bank (with the tree in front), the Necessity Store, Ginnings Hardware, Amos Drug Store, and Stephen's Grocery.

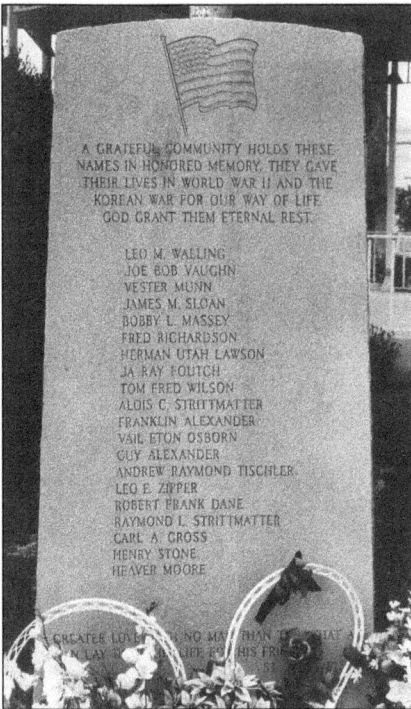

World War II claimed the lives of many young men in Pilot Point as it did in many towns across the United States. A grateful community erected this monument in 1954. (Courtesy of the *Pilot Point Post Signal*.)

The dedication of the World War II memorial in 1954 attracted people from not only Pilot Point but also the surrounding communities. The memory of the war was still fresh in the minds of the citizens, and the whole area came to honor the heroes. In the background looking north, the Farmer's and Merchant's Bank building is on the left with the north side of the square in the center.

Counter girl Ruby Ray smiles at customers at Doc (Carl) Amos's drugstore soda fountain about 1948. Doc's fountain and store was a popular hangout for the high school students after school and on Saturdays. (Courtesy of Ruby Ray.)

Yarbrough Grocery and Market was on the town square's south side. It was opened in 1945 by Dorothy and M. B. Yarbrough and was one of the many groceries on the square in the 1950s. M. B. is shown here behind the counter in about 1954. (Courtesy of Dorothy Yarbrough.)

Next to Yarbrough Grocery on the east corner of the south side was the White Auto Store, a franchise owned and operated by Clifton and Nadene Irick. Rural co-op electricity came to the outlying areas of Denton County in the late 1940s, and Clifton Irick prepared for this demand of products. In the first years of the 1950s, he sold electric refrigerators, washing machines, and radios to almost every farm family in the area. His financing plan with $3 down and 25¢ per week just couldn't be beat.

City employee Billy Bridges (left) and public works director Nealous Cockrill (center) place a new street sign at the corner of Liberty and Washington Streets. Pilot Point mayor for 20 years, J. Winston "Crack" Peel observes. In the upper right background are the opera house and the Queen Theatre on the west side of the square. This image is from 1951.

This building was the home of the local Church of the Nazarene in Pilot Point for many years after the main offices of the church moved. This photograph is from 1958; shortly after it was taken, the building was sold and moved. It was located just south of the Nazarene Monument.

Standing in front of the St. James Baptist Church, the Sledge family is pictured here in 1954. From left to right are Eli Sledge, his mother, Martha, and brothers, Larjulies and William. (Courtesy of Eli Sledge.)

The economy of Pilot Point in the 1940s and 1950s was under the control of these three men. J. Earl Selz (left) was the president of the Pilot Point National Bank. In the center is Lee Massey, owner of the Massy Cotton Gin, the largest industry in the area. J. Winston Peel (right) was the mayor of Pilot Point from the 1930s until the late 1950s. Between the three of them, they controlled the economic, political, and financial strings in Pilot Point.

Each year, the Pilot Point Chamber of Commerce awarded a $50 check to the farmer who brought in the first bale of cotton to the Massey Gin. In the photograph shown here, Joe Spratt (second from right) receives the check from Clyde Hall, president of the chamber. C. E. Hudspeth (far left), manager of the gin, and Mayor Clifton Irick observe. This is from the 1963 growing season.

The Pilot Point Volunteer Fire Department was composed entirely of business and civic leaders in the 1950s. This image taken in front of the fire station in 1951 shows, from left to right, (first row) Morris Usry (newspaper), Don Stephens (grocer), Nealous Cockrill (water department), Bill Ray, Jiggs Ray, Clifton Irick (appliance store), Frank Wilson (community power company), and Billy Bridges (city); (second row) Buster Wood (gasoline dealer), Lamar Whitley (dry cleaner), Billy Hilz (machine shop), Porter Gentry, George Hall, Omar Jones, Glen Beaty, Chief Alvin Branum, and Mike Amen.

It was a proud moment for P. C. Gentry in 1951 when he joined the Pilot Point Volunteer Fire Department. Fire chief Alvin Branum pins the badge on his shirt and welcomes him to the brotherhood. Branum, owner of a dry goods store, served as fire chief in Pilot Point for over 25 years. Most of the downtown businessmen served in the department in the 1950s. (Courtesy of the *Pilot Point Post Signal*.)

Rev. John Roberts and wife, Grace, of Rest Cottage join with Mayor Clifton Irick in ringing the Franklin College bell to celebrate the 50th anniversary of the founding of the Church of the Nazarene. In 1908, the Nazarene church was founded in Pilot Point when three groups joined forces to establish a new denomination. The anniversary was celebrated in 1958 when over 5,000 members of the Nazarene faith converged on Pilot Point in mass pilgrimage.

The photograph above shows the actual founding of the Nazarene church in 1908. A large tent was erected on the grounds of the old Franklin College, which then had been purchased by Rev. J. P. Roberts to establish Rest Cottage Rescue Home. Groups of believers from New England, California, and the South met to form a new Pentecostal holiness religion, and the result was the Church of the Nazarene. The image below shows the 75th anniversary when the granite monument was dedicated to mark the site.

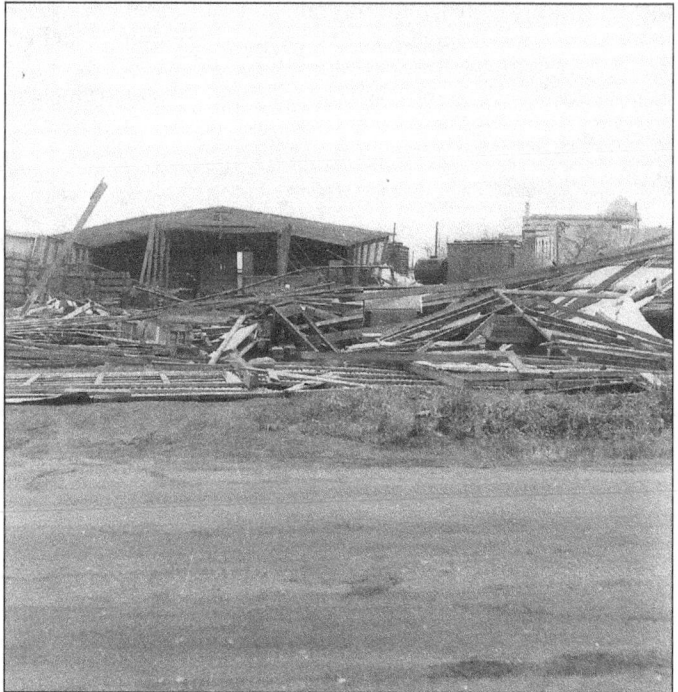

A devastating tornado touched down on the Pilot Point Town Square on April 6, 1955. The south side of the square was hit the hardest, with the Queen Theatre being almost destroyed. The photograph above shows the damage to the theater and hardware store. Warehouses located to the southwest of the square were also destroyed, as seen at right. The tornado came about 4:30 a.m. and "everyone was woke up by the noise which shook us out of bed," as reported by Clifton Irick, an eyewitness. "After daylight, we all went down there to see what happened and this is what we found." (Courtesy of Ruby Ray.)

In October 1956, the Pilot Point Volunteer Fire Department celebrated its 50th anniversary. It was a two-day affair with parades, games, dinner, and an awards ceremony. The parade featured all of the equipment, including the old hose reel from 1910 and the Model A fire truck, in addition to fire trucks from neighboring communities. Marie Beck presented a large centerpiece with a money tree floral arrangement to Chief Alvin Branum from Beck's Funeral Home. The parade is shown here passing in front of Alvin Branum's Dry Goods Store, which also doubled as the office of the Pilot Point Chamber of Commerce. (Courtesy of the late Kenneth Yarbrough.)

The old hose reel purchased in 1910 leads off the Firemen's Parade for the anniversary celebration. The old Model A fire truck purchased in 1922 follows it. In the left background, Sharkey Ray's Mobil station can be seen as the parade goes west on Liberty Street in 1956. (Courtesy of the late Kenneth Yarbrough.)

The north side of the square is the background for the fire department's anniversary parade in this photograph. The flatbed truck is loaded with the ladies from the 19th Century Club, who came to help celebrate the occasion. (Courtesy of the late Kenneth Yarbrough.)

PROGRAM

50th Anniversary Celebration

of

Pilot Point Fire Department

September 2 & 3, 1956

SUNDAY, SEPT. 2

1:00 P.M.	Registration Begins
2:30 P.M.	Quartet, Kennard Bros. from Fort Worth
4:00 P.M.	Hose Hookup Races
4:30 P.M.	Water Fight
6:00 P.M.	Refreshments for Ex-Firemen and Local Firemen and Families

MONDAY, SEPT. 3

9:30 A.M.	Parade at the Sound of the Siren
11:00 A.M.	Assembly at the Community Building
Master of Ceremonies	Chief Alvin Branum
Invocation	Rev. Charles Wages
Welcome Address	Mayor J. Winston Peel
Response	
Speaker	Supt. Ben Smith
Entertainment	School Band
	Richard Bryan, Director

Recess for Barbecue Luncheon.

The 50th anniversary of the fire department in Pilot Point drew large crowds for the two-day event. The program from September 2 and 3, 1956, lists the schedule for all the activities. It featured firemen from various departments in the area competing in water fights and races. (Author's collection.)

From left to right, Agnes Gibbs, Ernestine Tipton, and Arlie Tipton are shown in the photograph at right. Arlie and Ernestine Tipton opened Tipton's Café on the north side of the square in the 1940s. After many successful years of restaurant operation, they purchased the old Commercial Hotel just off the southwest corner of the square and opened the Tipton Hotel and Dining Room. The hotel had a large bell on the front porch, and every day at noon, Ernestine would ring the bell to let the town know that lunch was ready. Ernestine was well known for her perpetual pots of chili and vegetable soup. The house specialty was called a "mixed bowl," which was half chili and half soup.

Amos Drug Store on the east side of the town square was a place where people could meet and have a soda or cup of coffee and talk about local politics, events, or happenings. It was especially popular with the young people growing up in the 1950s. (Courtesy of Ruby Ray.)

Minnie and Carl "Doc" Amos are shown here standing behind the drug counter in this photograph from July 1954. Their young helpers, Robbie Fischer (far right) and Ruby Ray (second from right), were always on the job with a friendly smile for all the customers. Doc was quite well known for his off-the-cuff medical advice and the big cigar he always had going. (Courtesy of Ruby Ray.)

In the 1960s, everyone began to modernize their businesses. Grocery man M. B. Yarbrough was no exception. M. B. and his younger brother Kenneth (left) proudly show the new meat market in Yarbrough Grocery here. The new updates featured new refrigerated produce bins, modern shelving, and checkout stands, as well as a new meat market. Yarbrough Grocery closed in 1986 after 41 and a half years of operation. (Courtesy of Dorothy Yarbrough.)

This photograph shows the buildings on east Main Street just east of the town square. A pool hall and a restaurant occupied them. At the far end is the Ryan Motor Company building, home to the first Ford dealership in Pilot Point. The building was empty when this was taken in 1961.

On July 4, 1960, the state of Hawaii was admitted to the Union. The new 50-star American flag was flown in Pilot Point for the first time on that day. This picture, taken on that day, looks west to show the Massey Ford Company dealership that occupied the old opera house building. The darker brick building on the right was the Queen Theatre, which had been closed for several years when this photograph was made.

It was an exciting two days in November 1967 when the Warner Brothers bus pulled into town with Warren Beatty, Faye Dunaway, Michael Pollard, Estelle Parsons, and Gene Hackman. Everyone in town turned out to watch the filming of the Academy Award–winning motion picture *Bonnie and Clyde*. Portions of the street were closed down, and the traffic signal was removed for the filming. Bleachers were set up on the square, and the school kids took a holiday to watch Hollywood in Pilot Point. (Courtesy of Bob Brown.)

Dressed in 1930s attire and armed with Thompson machine guns, Faye Dunaway and Warren Beatty dash for the getaway car, Barrow's famous 1932 Ford. The Farmer's and Merchant's Bank, which had closed in 1930 and remained virtually unchanged, provided a unique setting for the movie. In the photograph below, Faye Dunaway is shown taking a break from filming as she and her assistant make their way to their trailer. The film premiered at the Campus Theater in Denton, Texas, in 1968. (Courtesy of Bob Brown.)

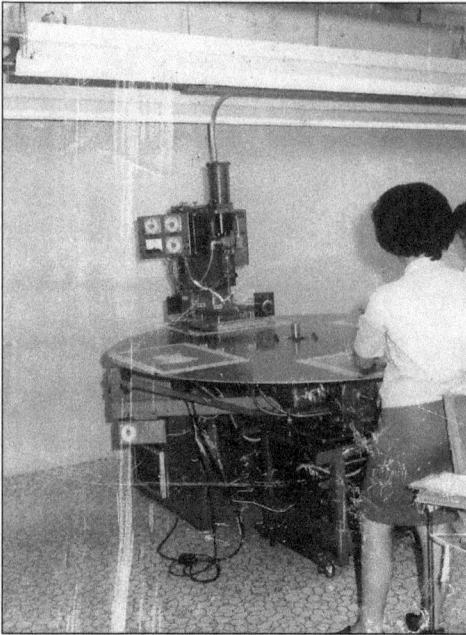

A major employer for women workers in Pilot Point in the 1960s was the Russell-Newman Manufacturing Company. The plant turned out ladies' lingerie. Many girls went to work here as their first job right after high school. The girl in the picture is Vera Jo Cordell, operating a large sewing machine. The people in town referred to the plant as "the panty factory." (Courtesy of Vera Cordell.)

Looking northwest in about 1955, the buildings on the west side can be seen. In the early days, these were home to Evans Dry Goods and Hardware. The post office was located there in the 1930s and 1940s. At the time of this picture, the buildings were mostly cafés and pool halls.

This aerial view of the downtown area of Pilot Point is from about 1960. In the bottom center of the picture, the large opera house building is seen. Left of that building is the Queen Theatre, followed by the buildings that were torn down in the 1970s. In the center left, behind the Pilot Point Bank building, the old IOOF Lodge Hall is pictured. It was also destroyed in the 1970s. The grassy circle in the center of the square has been there since the 1880s.

Former mayor and local historian Clifton Irick is show here in 1983 with two historic buildings in Pilot Point. In the foreground is the Masonic Hall, built in 1870, and in the background the Methodist church, built in 1910. Neither of these buildings would last more than a year after this photograph. The Methodist church burned to the ground in 1984, and the Masonic Hall was torn down shortly afterward.

The Gracie Home was one of the grandest mansions in Pilot Point (see page 59) around the dawn of the 20th century. In 1964, the property was acquired by the Pilot Point National Bank and demolished to make way for the new bank building. Pilot Point National Bank had previously been located on the square since its beginning in 1884. The new bank opened its doors on September 14, 1965. The bank remained at this location until 1990, when a new building was constructed on Highway 377. The building was given to the City of Pilot Point and is now the Community Library.

U.S. Congressman Ray Roberts secured the funding for a $288 million water reservoir in North Texas in the 1970s. In June 1982, construction of the lake dam was begun under the direction of Phillips and Jordan, Inc., of Knoxville, Tennessee. The Lake Ray Roberts Dam was to impound water from the Elm Fork of the Trinity River and create a watershed for the city of Dallas and other communities. Five years later on Tuesday, June 30, 1987, the gates were closed, and the Elm Fork began to back up and form a pool that would become one of the largest lakes in Texas. At the ceremony in Denton, Congressman Roberts said, "I am humbled to note that my name is worth a dam . . . and a reservoir."

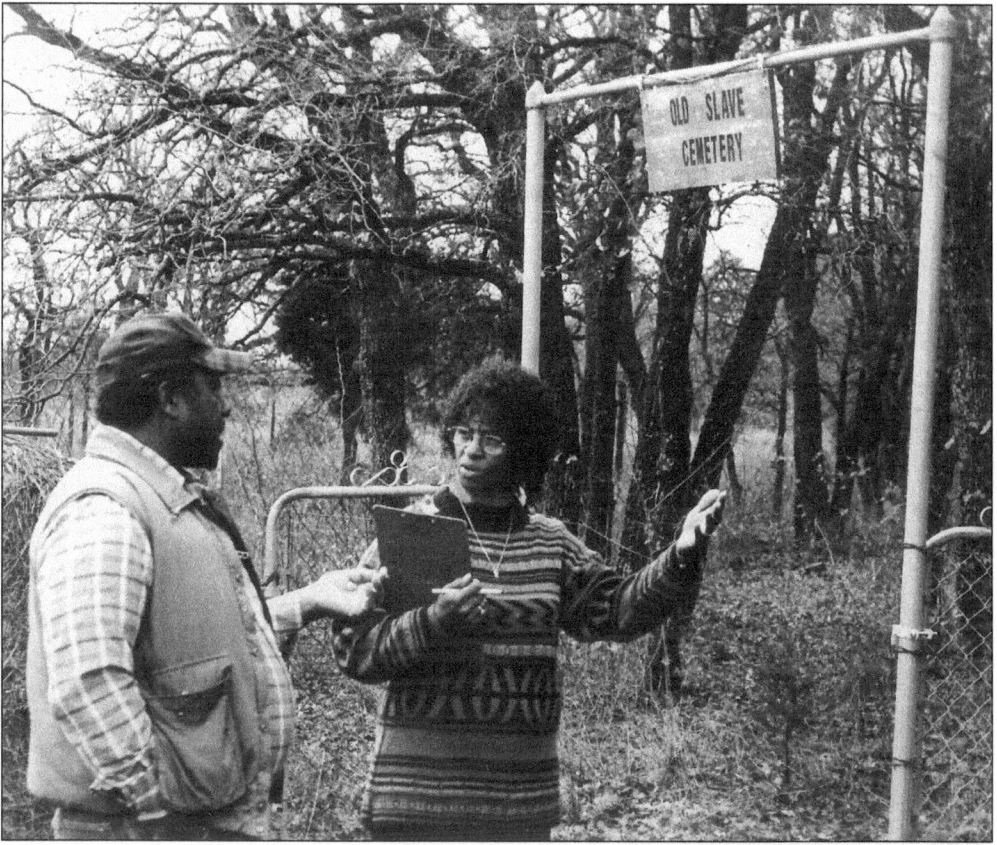

In 1998, a group of citizens restored a very old black cemetery just south of Pilot Point. Headstones were uncovered and set right, overgrown brush was cut, and an entrance sign was put on the gate. Former city council members Arthur Jackson and Pearly Mae Simpson discuss the history of the Old Slave Cemetery in this picture. (Courtesy of the *Pilot Point Post Signal*.)

Sam Allen was born a slave in the 1850s. After emancipation, he bought 50 acres of farmland east of Pilot Point and raised his large family. Allen's grandson, Eli Sledge, helped to restore the Old Slave Cemetery in 1998. (Courtesy of Eli Sledge.)

In this photograph, Eli Sledge is shown placing a picture of his aunt Analiza Holloway on the headstone of her husband. Henry Holloway was born into slavery in 1854 and was buried in 1916. (Courtesy of the *Pilot Point Post Signal*.)

This is the photograph of Analiza Holloway that Eli Sledge is placing on the gravestone in the image above. (Courtesy of Eli Sledge.)

In 1983, the Church of the Nazarene commemorated the 75th anniversary of the founding of their denomination by planting of a tree on the site of the marker. Clifton Irick, whose aunt and uncle were original founders of the church, was the guest speaker. (Courtesy of the *Pilot Point Post Signal*.)

In 1986, the State of Texas celebrated 150 years of independence. Many communities held special events for the occasion. The citizens of Pilot Point decided to build something lasting, and so funds were raised to construct a gazebo on the town square. Built entirely from private donations, the gazebo became a symbol and landmark of the old downtown. (Courtesy of the *Pilot Point Post Signal*.)

Carolyn Boerner was the city administrator in Pilot Point from 1992 until her death in 2003. Behind her is the old bank building, which was city hall when this photograph was made in the mid-1990s. It was her dream to revitalize the town square, and she was instrumental in securing a Main Street City designation for Pilot Point in 2002. (Courtesy of the *Pilot Point Post Signal*.)

124

Fall festivals are a tradition for downtown Pilot Point dating back quite a few years. This image from about 1971 shows the west side of the square during one of these celebrations. At the end of the street on the far left is the old Commercial Hotel, later the Tipton Hotel. Next to that building on the right is the old *Pilot Point Post Signal* newspaper office. The Ford dealership is on the corner and is followed by the opera house building, Queen Theatre, and a cabinet shop in the far right building.

When the World War II memorial was erected in 1954, several names were inadvertently omitted. This was corrected on Memorial Day 1999, when two new smaller markers were added. Friends of Freedom, a local patriotic organization, raised the money and purchased additional markers to include not only those left off in 1954 but also soldiers lost to Korea and Vietnam. In this photograph, the American Legion honor guard is on the right. From left to right are Lonnie Simmons, Bill Keith, Roy Timms, Nickie Simmel, Ronnie Alexander, and Mike Davis. (Courtesy of the *Pilot Point Post Signal*.)

Pilot Point takes it sports seriously. No matter what sport one is talking about, there is a winning tradition in the community. Pilot Point football teams have won the state championship two times and have won district, regional, and quarterfinal championships 24 times. The school is in the National High School Football record book for seven top records. Shown above are Adam Green, No. 35, and Ryan DeJernett, No. 30, who was state MVP in 1998. Coach G. A. Moore of Pilot Point has the most wins of any coach in Texas High School football history. (Courtesy of the *Pilot Point Post Signal.*)

The girls take their basketball just as seriously, having won championships seven times. (Courtesy of the *Pilot Point Post Signal.*)

Visit us at
arcadiapublishing.com